The World Book Library of Wildlife

A Chanticleer Press Edition
*Although this book was previously published as part of*
The Audubon Society Book of Wild Animals, *this edition is sponsored*
*exclusively by World Book-Childcraft International, Inc.*

# The World Book of
# Big Cats and
# Other Predators

*by Les Line and Edward Ricciuti*

World Book-Childcraft International, Inc.

A Subsidiary of the Scott & Fetzer Company
Chicago   London   Sydney   Tokyo   Toronto

Library of Congress Cataloging in Publication data:
Line, Les
The World Book of Big Cats and Other Predators.
"A Chanticleer Press edition."

ISBN 0-7166-2301-3 (volume 1)
World Book Library of Wildlife ISBN 0-7166-2300-5 (the set)
Library of Congress Catalog Card Number: 81-52956

Originally published in 1977 by Harry N. Abrams, Incorporated,
New York, as part of *The Audubon Society Book of Wild Animals*.

Prepared and produced by Chanticleer Press, Inc.
Printed in the United States.

Cover photograph by Russ Kinne/National Audubon Society
Collection/Photo Researchers, Inc.

*Note on Illustration Numbers: All illustrations are numbered according
to the pages on which they appear.*

First frontispiece. *A young male leopard* (Panthera pardus) *rests during
a trek through the jungle of Sri Lanka.* (George Holton)

Second frontispiece. *Speedster of the North American prairies, the
coyote* (Canis latrans) *can run 40 miles an hour. Although it is blamed
by ranchers for killing sheep, its primary diet consists of rabbits and
rodents.* (Jonathan Wright/Bruce Coleman, Inc.)

# Contents

At first glance, a cheetah bounding over the African plains in pursuit of a gazelle seems to have little in common with a huge blue whale cruising swiftly through the water in the middle of the ocean. But despite their great differences, these two mammals are variations on a single theme. Both are predators, animals that survive by eating other animals.

Modern ecologists define the word "predator" in a very broad way, so that even plant-eating animals are termed "leaf predators" or "seed predators." But for most of us, the word calls instantly to mind the flesh-eating mammals that are the subject of this volume. Superbly adapted for pursuing and capturing their prey, and living lives that are often full of danger and violence, these predatory mammals are the creatures that seem most vividly to illustrate Charles Darwin's "struggle for existence."

The land-dwelling predators in this book—the weasels, dogs, cats, bears and their relatives—are members of a single group of mammals known as the Order Carnivora. All of the carnivores, from the tiny, five-inch least weasel of North America to the 10-foot Kodiak bear of coastal Alaska, possess weapons for subduing their prey. Chief among these weapons are the long, sharp canine teeth, found in all carnivores including the dogs from which these teeth derive their name.

Nearly all of the marine mammals are also predators. The seals and their allies are closely related to the carnivores, and have clearly evolved from them. The leopard seal of Antarctic waters is as ferocious as its land-dwelling namesake. The whales, porpoises and dolphins are not related to the carnivores, but are

# Foreword

predators nonetheless; among the animals they hunt are seals, fish, seabirds, and even shrimp and other tiny marine animals, which they strain out of the water in huge quantities. Only one group of marine mammals, the dugongs and manatees, are not predatory. These peaceful animals feed on plants, but we have included them in this book because aside from their food habits, their way of life has much in common with that of the rest of the marine mammals.

Millions of years of evolution have produced a variety of ways of making a living as a hunter, so that today each of the many kinds of predators is specialized for hunting in its own way. But perhaps more than any other animals, the flesh-eaters have had trouble adjusting to life in a world dominated by man. Hunted as trophies or for their fur, pursued by fleets of whaling ships, shot when they prey on livestock, and driven from their habitat by the clearing of forests, many of the predators are now perilously close to extinction. Only by setting aside wild places, like those in which many of the pictures in this book were taken, can we preserve these splendid animals for future generations to enjoy.

In the white silence of a winter woodland, a sinuous pursuit ends lethally, as with blurring speed a long-tailed weasel rockets into a fleeing cottontail and kills it with a quick thrust of needle-sharp teeth to the brain. High in a tree overlooking a wooded savanna in Africa, a honey badger, flat and brutish of face, rakes open a beehive with its hooked foreclaws and gorges on the soft pupae and the sweet contents of the combs. On the windswept high plains of the Andes, a hog-nosed skunk shuffles among the sparse vegetation, naked snout searching the ground for insects to eat. The weasels and their relatives, collectively known as the mustelid family, are among the most diverse of all the carnivores in the myriad ways they exploit their surroundings to make a living. The forests, deserts, waters, and plains of all the continents except Australia and Antarctica are inhabited by one or another of the seventy species in this group, a family characterized by a low-slung body build and by scent glands that produce a rank, even vile, odor.

The members of the weasel clan also share several other traits, notably astonishing strength for their size, tenacious ferocity, and lethal agility. It is these qualities that are responsible for the group's multi-faceted success. Their fearlessness, murderous persistence, and power are legendary. The wolverine *(Gulo gulo)*, at fifty pounds, is perhaps the strongest of all mammals for its size. Fond of carrion, it chases cougars and even bears from their kills. When it needs fresh meat, the wolverine—which since the ice ages has retreated to the northern high country and the Arctic fringes—sometimes kills moose

# The Weasel Clan

and elk mired in snow. Deer caught in heavy snow occasionally are the prey of the North American fisher *(Martes pennanti)*, a dozen pounds of speed and ferocity, which is also the bane of porcupines. Once it corners a porcupine, a fisher performs like a lightweight boxer. It dances and it feints, dodging the crippling blows of the porcupine's quilled tail, and darting in to repeatedly slash the porcupine's unprotected face. When the porcupine is helpless and dying, the fisher overturns it and tears open its soft underparts.

The African striped weasel *(Poecilogale albinucha)* fences in a similar fashion with venomous snakes, waiting until the reptiles are exhausted before biting into the back of their heads. The badger *(Meles meles)* of Eurasia will squirm around inside its baggy but tough skin and bite back viciously if a dog grabs it by the scruff of the neck. With a grating snarl, it explodes from its burrow to assault trespassers upon its territory, especially in the breeding season. Animals as large as the African buffalo have been fatally wounded by the honey badger *(Mellivora capensis)*, which shreds their groin and genitals from below. Such courage and savagery are typical of the weasel clan, and even the smallest members, such as the least weasel *(Mustela ruxosa)*, which weigh only a few ounces, have held their ground when men have approached them on a kill.

The manner in which weasels *(Mustela)* make their kill is a chilling exercise in relentlessness. Like a slim missile homing in on a target, a long-tailed weasel *(M. frenata)* will match every evasive twist and turn of a rodent or hare, as though linked to its prey by an invisible strand. Almost invariably, the chase ends with a fatal strike at the base of the victim's skull, or the neck, often delivered with blinding speed. The lithe, slender body of the weasel enables it to prowl the underground burrows of rodents with almost serpentine ease. Virtually anywhere a weasel can wedge its pointed black snout, it can take its body. Mice are tracked to the ends of their burrows, and knotholes serve as entrances to henhouses. Once inside, the weasel may slaughter as many hens as it can reach, but not because it is particularly bloodthirsty. When a weasel is confined with an abundance of prey, its highly tuned predatory responses may be difficult to shut down, and it may be unable to stop killing as long as the prey is moving.

Even trees offer no escape for the fleeing victim of a weasel, for it will go aloft after its dinner. Many members of the clan, in fact, display the same lightness of foot in the branches as on the ground. The martens *(Martes)* do most of their hunting in the trees and subsist largely on squirrels. The tayra *(Tayra barbara)*, a yard-long beast of the American tropics, takes to the trees to hunt arboreal anteaters and steal bananas. If pursued by men with dogs, as is likely after a raid on a banana plantation, the tayra may use the forest canopy as a highway. Even the ground-dwelling ferret badger *(Melogale moschata)* of Formosa sometimes forsakes its burrow to sleep cradled in the boughs.

Of all environments, however, the one in which the mustelids truly surpass the other carnivores is in the water. The river otters *(Lutra)* and the minks—*Mustela vison* of North America and *M. lutreola* of Eurasia—manage the weasel-like dazzling maneuvers in the water, as they swim with supple grace and swiftness after fish. They have established a virtual monopoly over the role of freshwater mammalian predator. And two of the mustelids even have followed evolutionary paths which have led to the sea, specifically the Pacific Ocean. The small marine otter *(Lutra felina)* catches fish and other seafood where the chill waters of the Humboldt Current sweep close to the west coast of South America, from northern Peru south. However, the marine otter still retains substantial links with land, for it eats its catch ashore and dens there. The endangered giant otter *(Pteronura braziliensis)* of South America is the longest—six feet from snout to tip of tail. Weighing hardly more than an ounce, the least weasel is the bantam among the group and, in fact, is the smallest carnivore.

Big and small, mustelids have highly developed scent glands whose secretions range in potency from slightly pungent to overpowering. The skunks, of course, are notorious for the chemical warfare they wage on their enemies. Some of their mustelid relatives, however, are just as odorous. The green secretion shot by the aptly named Malayan stink badger *(Mydaus javanensis)* is supposedly potent enough to asphyxiate dogs which receive a substantial dose. The odor given off by the marbled polecat *(Vormela peregusna)* of Eurasia and the African zorille *(Ictonyx striatus)* is also devastating. Most of the mustelids wear some sort of contrasting blotches or stripes which warn other beasts to give them a wide berth. As a rule, the more powerful their chemical defense, the more vivid their markings.

The impact of such weapons has not been lost on humans. Witness the epithets inspired by such creatures as skunks and polecats. As a group, in fact, the mustelids probably have been associated with more unsavory human actions than any other mammals. At the same time, they have been among the most prized of creatures, valued so greatly for their furs that men have risked their lives in the wilderness to trap them. Ermine, the winter white-coated weasel, was once reserved for royalty. Marten, commercially known as sable, and mink are still reserved largely for the wealthy. What is most priceless about the members of the weasel clan, however, is their magnificent savagery, symbolic of a wild world that is rapidly becoming only a memory.

**13.** *At home in every kind of land habitat from southern Canada into South America, the long-tailed weasel* (Mustela frenata) *is a super predator in a small and attractive package. No more than sixteen inches long, it is normally chocolate brown with a yellowish belly, but in northern areas it turns pure white in winter—except for a black tip on its six-inch tail. Furriers call winter weasel pelts "ermine," and in medieval Europe they were reserved for the garments of royalty; 50,000 skins of the short-tailed weasel or stoat were used for the coronation of King George VI of Great Britain in 1937. Such variable beauty disguises a fierce hunter of squirrels, rabbits, snakes, frogs, insects, songbirds, and a multitude of mice and rats. Indeed, the weasel has been accused, not without cause, of killing just for fun; a weasel that finds itself in a henhouse, for instance, may slaughter dozens of chickens in a single night. One scientist called it "the most blood-thirsty of all animals," adding that "its favorite drink is warm blood sucked from the neck of its prey." And a weasel will not hesitate to attack a man who gets in its way. But this petite killer is not without its own mortal enemies: hawks, owls, and even prowling house cats.*
(Kenneth Fink)

**4-15.** *In a remarkable sequence of photographs, a long-tailed weasel fights a cottontail rabbit in the snowy mountain forests of Wyoming and launches an attack with blurring speed almost too fast for the human eye to follow. Although the rabbit is many times larger than the weasel, its size gives it no advantage over its bantam adversary, and the outcome of the pursuit is inevitable. Like a slim white missile homing on a target, the weasel stays with its chosen victim as it frantically twists and turns in the snow, finally seizing the cottontail at the base of the skull and sinking needle-sharp teeth into the brain. The hunt ended, the seven-ounce weasel drags the three-pound rabbit off into the forest.* (Fred and Doris Burris)

**16** *top. An American badger (Taxidea taxus) devours a rattlesnake. Using its powerful front legs, which are armed with long claws, as well as its strong jaws, a badger can dig a hole in the ground, vanish, and plug the burrow behind it in a few seconds. The badger's coarse fur once was used to make shaving brushes.* (Charles G. Summers/Amwest)

**17.** *Although they are lovely to look at, the skunks of the New World are not animals to be disturbed. An arched white-plumed tail is a fair warning to intruders that the skunk is prepared to spray—with remarkable accuracy—a foul-smelling fluid that burns the eyes and whose acrid odor persists for days. Most frequently encountered is the striped skunk (Mephitis mephitis), which has the distressing habit of taking up residence beneath suburban homes and summer cabins.* (John Ebeling)

**18** *overleaf. Four feet long, weighing perhaps fifty pounds, and suggesting a small bear, the wolverine (Gulo gulo) fears no other creature. It will kill an elk or moose struggling in deep snow, drive a mountain lion or grizzly bear away from its meal, attack a bear cub, and rob man's traplines. The wolverine roams the tundra and subarctic forests around the pole; a male wolverine requires a territory of about 1000 square miles, which he will share with two or three females.* (Jack Couffer/Bruce Coleman, Inc.)

**16** *above. An inhabitant of streams, lakes, and tidal marshes across most of North America, the mink (Mustela vison) is a deadly hunter of muskrats. A mink will corner one of these big aquatic rodents in its bank burrow and quickly dispatch it; or rip open a muskrat's cattail lodge, devour the young, and then claim the house as its own den.* (Leonard Lee Rue III)

**16** *above. A large weasel that haunts the treetops and is equipped with strong claws for climbing and a long bushy tail to keep its balance, the American marten (Martes americana) pursues its favorite prey, the red squirrel, through conifer forests from Newfoundland to Alaska.* (Hans Reinhard/Bruce Coleman, Inc.)

Creeping low to the ground, its tail outstretched, its belly almost brushing the earth, the red fox stalks a cottontail. Slowly, sharp nose pointed in the rabbit's direction, it inches imperceptibly toward its prey. A dozen feet away it halts, still concealed by the undergrowth. Its body tenses, muscles bunch, and it explodes out of hiding, darting for its prey, which spurts away, with the fox in swift, silent pursuit.

On the prairie, speckled with flowers, a jackrabbit is running for its life. Behind it courses a coyote, jaws parted, teeth gleaming. Ahead, unknown to the rabbit, another coyote lies in wait, preparing for the kill.

Foam flying from its mouth and nostrils, a sambar deer flees across the landscape of southern Asia. Its flanks are bleeding, its hindquarters ripped open. With it runs terror, silent and tenacious, the dhole pack—wild dogs that are the scourge of the eaters of grass, leaves, and buds. The sambar still lives, but it will die as it runs.

The dog family (Canidae) consists of hunters generally built for the chase, although some members are sufficiently sly to catch prey by stealth. A few, generally only the smaller members of the group, are solitary hunters. The agile, intelligent red fox *(Vulpes vulpes)* prowls the land alone, as silently as a blown leaf, ready to run down a rabbit if necessary, but also eager to pounce upon a mouse that has stirred in the grass. In its hunting methods, it sometimes behaves more like a cat than a dog. The gray fox of North America *(Urocyon cinereoargenteus)* is also a lone hunter. Nightly, it fol-

# The Hunters: Dogs

ows the same route, a twisted, winding course over the countryside as it casts about for small rodents. Similarly, the coyote *(Canis latrans)* is prone to patrolling its territory over a regular hunting trail, night after night, even year after year. Yet for the coyote the hunt can also be a family affair, which is why coyotes, seldom exceeding thirty pounds, can sometimes kill prey that is bigger, stronger, and faster than they, and it is this aspect of their behavior that so strongly characterizes the group. The members of a coyote family will take turns running a pronghorn antelope in a circle until it falls from exhaustion, whereupon all the coyotes move in for the kill. The same tactic is used by the small golden jackal *(Canis aureus)* of Africa and Asia to occasionally catch deer and similar hoofed creatures.

At their most devastating the canine hunters work as highly organized, lethally efficient teams, ranging from two to a dozen or more members. Deep-chested, lean, and long of leg, the canine hunters are typified by their relentless pursuit, seemingly ruthless but actually entailing only the degree of violence necessary to make the kill. The evolution of team tactics among them has been accompanied by the growth of social organizations that are so sophisticated and complex they rival those of the most advanced primates. The technique of hunting as a group is most highly developed, and most harrowing to watch, among the wolves *(Canis lupus)*, African hunting dogs *(Lycaon pictus)*, and the dholes *(Cuon alpinus)* of Asia.

These creatures form hunting packs that operate with superb coordination, and regularly kill animals which easily could repel the attack of a single one of their number. African hunting dogs have been known to employ some members of their pack as decoys to distract the victims from the real assault. Wolf packs split up to separate a cow moose from her defenseless calf. A few members of the pack will drive the cow, harrying her so that gradually they split her from the calf, pressing her farther and farther from her offspring, while the remainder of the pack swarm over the helpless young.

The dholes, the feared "red dogs" of Kipling, sometimes engage in elaborate maneuvers, likened to beating the bush for game and running the prey that is flushed into a trap set by part of the pack.

Dholes hunt primarily by scent, an advantage in the thick cover they generally inhabit. Wolves and African hunting dogs, which often live in the open, hunt largely by eye, but if they are seeking prey in the forest or thick bush, they also nose about in an effort to pinpoint the location of their victim. Once it has been targeted, they sneak as close to it as possible before revealing themselves. Then there is a furious rush toward the prey, as the hunters try to bring it to bay before it can flee. Large targets, such as a large antelope, may stand their ground and fight, and more often than is generally believed, drive off their tormentors. But once the victim chooses to flee, the advantage is with the pack, which strings out in pursuit, sometimes running in relays, until exhaustion forces the hunted creature to stop. If the hunters are dholes, the quarry often is half dead before it stops running, for they harry their victims in a particularly gruesome manner. Running alongside, even under the quarry, the red dogs snap and tear at it with crippling bites, literally eating their victim alive as it flees.

Once the quarry of the pack has been brought to bay, the tactics used by all of the wild dogs are the same. If the prey is small, it is immediately overwhelmed in a flood of snarling bodies. Large victims are encircled by dancing, darting forms, trying from every direction for a telling bite. Wolves and African hunting dogs customarily try for a grip on the snout of the victim. When one of the pack has managed to hold fast, the rest attack the quarry from the rear, trying to get it to the ground.

As might be surmised, to cooperate so smoothly, packs must be highly structured and joined by strong communal ties. The pack is, then, a form of extended-family unit, which serves not only to provide food but for protection as well. Youngsters growing up within the pack benefit almost immediately from the ties that hold it together. Wolves and hunting dogs swallow chunks of flesh at the kill, then return to the young and regurgitate it for them to eat. Dholes sometimes form community nurseries, and it is thought that the females may share with each other some of the responsibilities of rearing the offspring.

The size of a pack varies from a few to more than two dozen members, but to work most effectively, it needs at least six animals. Groups of fewer than that are at a tremendous disadvantage, not only during the hunt, but also because they probably are not large enough for the development of the complex network of relationships that cement the pack together as a unit. The maximum size of the pack is rather flexible, for it is most likely linked to external conditions. Where food is abundant, and large prey abounds, the size of the pack can increase without some of its members going hungry after a kill. But if a pack is so large that even successful hunts leave many members still famished, it will break down, perhaps into two new hunting bands, which together can cover a much greater expanse of territory and thus multiply the food supply available to the same number of animals.

Thus, the hunting pack, as formed by wild canines, is a means of exploiting food that would seldom if ever be available, without the strength that comes from unity.

**25.** *No wild dog is found over such a wide variety of habitats as the dhole* (Cuon alpinus) *of India and Asia. Although primarily a forest dweller, it is equally at home along seashores and high on earth's greatest mountains, the Himalayas. It will feed on sea turtles, ripping off their shells, and drive mountain sheep over precipices. The "red dog," as it is often called, hunts in packs that may number thirty animals, but because it lacks the great speed of other canids it will doggedly follow a chosen victim—ibex, reindeer, wild boar, sambar—for hours before finally making the kill by grabbing the prey from behind or disemboweling it on the run. Also unlike many other wild dogs that hunt in packs, the dhole is relatively quiet, neither barking nor howling. Biologists report that the dhole hunts across vast territories and rarely makes more than one kill at a time in a particular area. They also note its fondness for the blossoms of wild rhubarb. Once widely distributed from Siberia south across China into Sumatra, Java, and India, the dhole is rare or extinct today over much of its historic range.* (Stanley Breeden)

**26-27.** *African wild dogs* (Lycaon pictus) *are famous among animal behaviorists for their highly organized social life. Packs of anywhere from a half-dozen to sixty wild dogs live as a close-knit community, and while there is no dominance hierarchy, responsibilities are strictly divided. While some dogs lead the hunt, pursuing wildebeests, warthogs, gazelles, and zebras across the savanna at speeds reach-* *ing 30 miles an hour, other members of the pack stand guard at the dens —usually old aardvark holes—where litters of six to eight pups are hidden. When the hunters return, they regurgitate partly digested meat to feed nursing females, young, and aged members of the pack.* (26 William and Marcia Levy/ National Audubon Society Collection/Photo Researchers, Inc.; 27 James Malcolm/Anthro-Photo)

28 *overleaf. A pack of wolves* (Canis lupus) *pursues a moose—unsuccessfully this time—in the deep snows of Isle Royale National Park, in Michigan. The wolves of this forty-mile-long wilderness preserve in Lake Superior are equally famous in research circles. Breeding wolves first reached Isle Royale in the late 1940s, crossing eighteen miles of ice from the Ontario shore.*

*Their unexpected arrival was nature's answer to a dilemma—a population of moose that, in the absence of any predator, had exploded and severely overbrowsed the forest. Today, two dozen wolves live on Isle Royale in careful balance with a moose herd that in midwinter averages a thousand animals. (Rolf Peterson)*

**30.** *Largest of all wild dogs, a wolf may stand thirty inches at the shoulders and weigh 150 pounds and is capable of bringing down prey as big as musk-oxen and caribou.* (John Ebeling)

**31.** *Falling snow dusts the thick pelt of a red fox* (Vulpes vulpes) *sleeping off a heavy meal. On Isle Royale in winter, scavenging foxes are a principal beneficiary of moose kills by the wolf pack.* (Durward L. Allen)

**32** *overleaf. The gray fox* (Urocyon cinereoargenteus) *of North and South America has remarkable habits for a member of the dog family: it climbs trees and likes to eat ripe fruit and grain.* (Leonard Lee Rue III)

Its passage heralded by the sharp yaps of the little muntjacs, or barking deer, a tiger walks the land. Moving fluidly, the massive muscles in its shoulders undulating to match its strides, it pads through a green tongue of woodland below a sunlit, grassy hillside. At the margin of the trees, the tiger pauses. The great, ruffed head turns slowly. The eyes, with chilling assurance, survey the landscape. Scattered in knots on the verdant slope ahead are sambar deer, large, big-eared creatures covered by coarse brown hair. They are feeding, their dark bodies gilded by the sun of the late afternoon. As the tiger scans the hillside, a wave of perturbation sweeps over the little clusters of deer. Heads are raised. Ears twitch. Nostrils quiver wetly, inquisitively, testing the soft breeze. The deer sense that, in the peace of the declining day, death has arrived.

The cats are many in species, diverse in size, but alike in mien and in that, from the largest, the 700-pound tiger *(Panthera tigris)* of Siberian snows, to the dainty margay *(Felis wiedii)* of South America, they are all killers. They live by killing, and the more efficiently they do it, the better the chances that their progeny will survive. It is the lot that has fallen to them in the natural scheme of things.

Adaptation to this end has conferred a terrible majesty upon some of them, especially the larger ones. It has made all of them sleek and silent, stealthy and supple, so that even the smallest seem to possess both an inscrutable cunning and vast dignity. It has armed them with muscles that can move fluidly but with sledge-

# The Hunters: Cats

hammer power, with fearsome teeth and hooked claws that can either hold a victim fast or rake the life from it. The cats need all of these advantages, for they face the unending task of killing enough prey to survive, and must surmount enormous obstacles to accomplish it.

Concealment, then a sudden bound or explosive rush, is favored by most of the feline hunters, but within the overall pattern the hunt takes many forms. A stealthy, solitary stalk is the way of most cats, both the smaller ones, such as the African wild cat *(Felis lybica)*, and their larger relatives. The tiger creeps to within a few yards of the victim, then launches its attack from the rear or the flank, fastening its claws into the body of the prey while it bites the neck. It can be an ambush, favored by the small clouded leopard *(Neofelis nebulosa)* of southern Asia and the more common Afro-Asian spotted leopard *(Panthera pardus)* and the American bobcat *(Felis rufus)*, which may drop upon their prey from a tree. The hunt sometimes takes the shape of a spectacular acrobatic performance, like the leaps of the slender, long-legged serval *(Felis serval)* of Africa. With blinding speed, it bounds through the high savanna grasses, flushing birds, and springing after them to claw them out of the air six feet above the ground.

Whatever the style of the hunt, however, success depends upon the ability to work close enough to the prey in secret so it can be brought down in a single, decisive maneuver. The nature of the maneuver depends upon the particular physical assets of the cat that performs it. The cougar *(Felis concolor)* of the Americas is fast enough to overtake a deer on a course of a hundred yards or so. Usually, however, the conditions under which the cougar hunts are far from ideal, so it tries to get within a few yards where it can strike like an uncoiled steel spring, hurtling into its victim and even bowling it over. The caracal *(Felis caracal)*, a sand-colored lynx of Africa and Asia, relies far more on its speed. With hind limbs longer than the fore, it can run down even gazelles over a short distance. For these and the other cats, the hunt is almost always a solitary affair, except when mothers are teaching their young the skills of the killer. A major exception to the rule, however, is the lion *(Panthera leo)*, most social of all the cats, the only one to live in large family groups, and as often as not a team hunter. Lions, or more precisely lionesses, regularly hunt as a group, with some members of the pride driving prey into the jaws of the others.

The strength of the cats, relative to size, is awesome. A leopard, which seldom weighs more than a man, commonly hauls prey almost as heavy as itself into a tree and stows it in the branches for a later meal. Cougars, about the weight of leopards, have dragged off horses many times heavier than themselves. Buffalo, gaur, wild boar, oryx, moose, caribou, elk—all but the very largest herbivores regularly fall prey to the bigger cats. The prey is often quite varied, however, proof of the adaptability of the group. Caimans in the water and monkeys in the trees furnish meals for the stocky, powerful jaguar *(Panthera onca)*, whose range extends from the tropics into the southwestern United States. Tigers sometimes rove the mangrove swamps at seaside in search of fish and even turtles. Lions occasionally pounce upon rats, in imitation of their smaller, domestic relatives. Few of the cats, in fact, cannot afford to be generalists in dietary matters when the need arises. Carrion almost always is acceptable, and sometimes sought out—not only by the aged and the sick but occasionally even by the strong. Lions regularly drive hyenas away from prey which those much-maligned night prowlers have downed in a legitimate chase.

While the cats are adaptable predators, some of them are sufficiently specialized to demonstrate how intimate are the bonds between victim and killer. The Canadian lynx *(Felis lynx)*, for example, depends mainly upon the big varying hare, or "snowshoe rabbit," for food. The hares undergo a cyclic rise and fall in their populations. At the peak of the cycle, approximately every seven years, they swarm over the landscape, but a year later they have all but vanished. The size of the lynx population parallels that of the hares, but always a year behind. The intimacy of the lynx's ties with the hare is demonstrated by the cat's large, snowshoe feet, which mirror those that carry the hare over the crusted snow.

The effects of specialization also are revealed in the body of the cheetah *(Acinonyx jubatus)*, which relies mainly upon small, fleet gazelles as prey. The cheetah, unlike the other cats, is built not so much for stealth as for speed. Its conformation in some ways approaches that of the wild dogs, which run down their prey rather than surprise it. This large, spotted cat has exceptionally long legs, and its claws, like those of the dogs, are blunt. The claws of the cheetah do not serve as weapons, so there is no need to keep them sharp. Moreover, unlike the other cats, which can sheathe their talons and turn their paws into velvet gloves, the cheetah can withdraw its claws only partly. When it hunts, it relies on its keen eyes and capacity for a sudden burst of speed—up to 70 miles an hour—which no other creature on four legs can match over a short distance. The only hope of the cheetah's prey is to twist and turn until the fleet cat tires and, sensing its limitations, gives up the chase. Often, evasive tactics are successful, and the cheetah is left panting and hungry. But when the hunt of the cheetah goes in its favor, the pursuit ends in a roil of dust and a welling of blood. It is a stark reminder that the purpose of the hunting beast is the cessation of life, but for a reason—so that other life can continue. It is symbolic of the endless cycle of death and renewal that is nature.

**39** *and* **40** *overleaf. There are
seven races of tigers scattered
sparsely about the Asian forests,
and all are considered to be
endangered. Indeed, the Bali tiger
is probably extinct, for it has not
been seen on that island since 1952.
Of some other races, less than a
hundred animals may survive. Most
numerous, if two thousand can be
considered numerous, is the Bengal
tiger* (Panthera tigris tigris) *of India.
This solitary hunter is the largest
cat on earth; a male may stand three
feet at the shoulders, measure thir-
teen feet in length including its tail,
and weigh 600 pounds. No animal is
immune to the tiger's great strength
—not even elephants, rhinoceroses,
gaurs, or crocodiles—and a tiger
may claim a kill from a leopard. Its
appetite is voracious: a healthy tiger
requires three tons of meat a year,
the equivalent of thirty domestic
cattle or seventy axis deer. But its
meals do not come easy. To make a
kill, a tiger must stalk to within a
few feet of the victim, then bring it
down with a final lunge. If it misses,
the cat may chase the prey a hundred yards or so, but with little
chance of catching it. Thus the tiger
often augments its diet with more
easily obtained fish, frogs, turtles,
rodents, even locusts. Tigers readily
take to water, swimming with ease
across swift rivers, large lakes,
or bays. (39* Stanley Breeden;
*40* Rajesh Bedi)

**42** *below. Named for the German naturalist Peter Simon Pallas, who was noted for his scientific explorations of Russia and Siberia in the eighteenth century, Pallas' cat (Felis manul) has small ears and long fur on its flanks, belly, and tail—adaptations for life in the cold, snowy steppes of central Asia.* (Tom McHugh/National Audubon Society Collection/Photo Researchers, Inc.)

**42** *below. Enemy of snakes in the tropical American rain forests, an ocelot (Felis pardalis) can dispatch even a large boa constrictor. Male and female ocelots hunt in cooperative fashion, meowing to one another like house cats, and they share in rearing the young.* (Loren McIntyre)

**42** *below. Big, round ears that almost touch identify the serval (Felis serval) of Africa's woodland savannas. Resembling a scaled-down cheetah, the serval has long, slender forelegs that it uses to probe rocky crevices and dens in search of rodents.* (Edward S. Ross)

*below. Cautiously stalking the ·y grasslands, savannas, and bush ·untry of Africa and southern sia, the caracal (Felis caracal) ·eys on rodents, hares, ostriches, ·d small antelopes. It will leap ·to a low-flying flock of birds to ·ing down several at a time. This ·re desert relative of the lynx ·ce was trained to hunt game for ·an. (Francis Petter/Jacana)*

**43** *below. Hunter of northern forests around the world, the lynx (Felis lynx) has huge, hairy feet that enable it to travel over deep snow without sinking. In Canada, the life of the lynx is inexorably tied to the snowshoe hare, its chief prey; the hare population is cyclic, and when it plunges every seven years, lynx numbers likewise suffer a severe decrease. (Edward R. Degginger)*

**43** *below. The cougar (Felis concolor) once stalked the New World wilderness from the Atlantic to the Pacific, from northern Canada almost to the tip of South America. Hunted as a game trophy, persecuted as a killer of livestock, intolerant of civilization, the cougar has vanished from most of its historic haunts. Weighing 200 pounds, it can easily bring down a large deer and lug the carcass back to its den. (Maurice Hornocker)*

*4 overleaf. Prey of the bobcat ·Felis rufus) runs the gamut from ·ttle deer mice to adult deer. ·rowing to twenty-five pounds of ·uscle and sinew, the bobcat—its ·rademark is its tail, which appears ·o have been bobbed—hunts the ·rests, swamps, and deserts of ·Jorth America from coast to coast, ·nd from the Canadian border deep ·nto Mexico. It exists surprisingly ·lose to towns and cities, but ·umans are rarely aware of its ·resence except during the mating ·eason, late in the winter, when the*

*bobcat rends the nighttime silence with frightening squalls and yowls. Conservationists fear for the future of the bobcat; since the luxury fur trade was denied the skins of endangered spotted cats, its beautiful pelt has come into great demand and this has triggered heavy trapping pressure. (Mark Stouffer)*

**46** *second overleaf. Third largest of the world's cats, after the tiger and the lion, is the jaguar (Panthera onca), which ranges from Patagonia to the Mexico-United States border. Its name derives from an Indian word meaning "creature that overcomes its prey in a single bound," which tells much about the power of this 250-pound nemesis of deer, peccaries, and capybaras. Like the leopard, the jaguar has a melanistic color phase, but even in glossy black individuals the shadows of the spots are visible. (Loren McIntyre)*

**48-49.** *Lions* (Panthera leo) *are famous for the gentle and affectionate family life in a pride that may include two or three males, ten lionesses, and their young of varying ages. Male lions tolerate the rough romping and food stealing of the cubs, but there is a lot of noisy quabbling among adults over kills, and males often wrest food from their mates. After a meal, however, calm prevails. Lion cubs—two to four to a litter—weigh about three pounds at birth. They are weaned in three months and immediately begin taking hunting lessons from their mother. Young males must leave the pride at the age of three and a half years, but lionesses often remain for their entire lives. Wildebeests, zebras, and the ubiquitous little Thomson's gazelles are the usual prey of a pride. (48 top* Wolfgang Bayer; *48 bottom and 49 top* George Schaller/Bruce Coleman, Inc.; *49 bottom* M. Philip Kahl)

**50** *overleaf and* **52** *second overleaf. The cheetah* (Acinonyx jubatus) *is capable of incredible speed—nearly 70 miles an hour—but only in short bursts. If it fails to bring down its carefully selected target within about 600 yards, the pursuit is given up, for by then the cat is totally exhausted. Cheetahs prey most often on medium-sized antelopes, but they can bring down an animal as large as a young wildebeest, killing with a throat bite—then first eating the liver, kidneys, and heart.* (50 M. Philip Kahl; 52 Thomas Nebbia)

49

The hulking form shambles to the water's edge, wades in, and plops down on its rump. Sitting in a stream with the water up to its chest, an Alaskan brown bear seems to be giving an impression of a big, hairy man enjoying a bath. There is much about the bears, in fact, that encourages anthropomorphism, for in many of their mannerisms, including even their plantigrade style of walking, with the entire underpart of the foot touching the ground, they seem to caricature humans. It is, however, an illusion that is quickly dispelled when a bear is aroused. A combat between two Alaskan brown bears *(Ursus arctos)*, for example, is bone-chilling to witness, a battle between savage titans waged with the ultimate ferocity. Half-ton bodies no longer shuffle, but move explosively, almost lithely, with furious power. Piggy snouts quiver wetly and lips are drawn back to reveal huge canine fangs, yellowed and wickedly curved. Massive heads thrust forward or twist around to bury the fangs in matted brown hide, while the air resounds to thunderous snarls. Any anthropomorphic resemblances vanish in a scene of immense bestiality. The illusion, however, is persistent, and crops up again when an American black bear *(Ursus americanus)* stands up to beg for handouts in a national park or when a polar bear *(Ursus maritimus)* plunges with apparent joy from an ice cliff into the sea. The same sort of sham is carried on by certain members of another family of creatures, related to the bears and typified by the raccoon *(Procyon lotor)*. In the raccoon's case, it is the creature's appealing manner and especially the use of its forepaw which contribute most to the fancy that it is really a little

# Big Bears and Their Kin

round man in a fur suit. Outside of the other primates, few creatures have digits which so closely simulate human fingers in form and function. The resemblance was not lost upon the Algonquin Indians. The name "raccoon" comes from the Algonquian word *arough-coune*, which means "he who scratches with his hands." The "hands" of the raccoon are a marvel. It and its South American cousin the crab-eating raccoon *(P. cancrivorus)* have a wonderfully delicate touch, a sense so highly developed that they rely on it almost exclusively when dabbling in the shallows for crustaceans, fish, frogs, and other food.

Highly adaptable to human presence, the raccoon manages to exist even in cities, and thrives in suburbs, where the contents of backyard garbage cans provide an endless supply of food. Encountered while on a nocturnal foray into the trash can, a raccoon may pause with a purloined tidbit raised halfway to its mouth, and stare quizzically at the intruder as if to ask why it has been disturbed at its dining. At such times it can be a charming animal. If cornered by dogs, however, the raccoon displays another facet to its nature. It is transformed from a seemingly amiable clown into a ball of fighting fury. Cunning and tenacious, a raccoon is more than a match for a dog of its size—usually a dozen pounds but often much larger—as it crouches, comes in low, and aims for the throat. The raccoon's long, lean relatives the coatis *(Nasua)* can prove similarly difficult opponents for dogs, for they have especially long, sharp canine fangs which can slash through fur and flesh in one swift thrust.

The raids by raccoons on garbage cans testify to the omnivorous diet of these creatures, a trait shared by other members of its family and most bears. Coatis, ranging in troops of from a few to dozens of animals, poke their long snouts into virtually every crack and cranny in their path, eating everything from fruit to small mammals. The ringtail cats (*Bassariscus astutus*), of Oregon to Central America, have a similarly varied diet, although they lean heavily on rodents and insects. Among the bears, the most specialized in terms of eating habits is the polar bear, for it spends most of its life on the ice or at sea, away from vegetation save an occasional strand of seaweed. The great white bear subsists almost entirely on flesh, mostly of seals, and has even been known to stalk humans on the ice in much the same way it hunts pinnipeds. Although the polar bear is the only one of its tribe that regularly kills large animals, most bears are capable of taking sizable prey. The Asiatic black bear (*Selenarctos thibetanus*), a 300-pound creature with a reputation for aggressiveness, will occasionally attack and kill cattle and sheep. So at times will the big brown bears, including the grizzly of North America, which can down prey the size of a bison. Generally, however, they prey on creatures no larger than rodents. In midsummer, the Alaskan browns—some of which weigh more than 1600 pounds, stand almost a dozen feet high, and are the largest living land carnivores—gather at streams where salmon spawn. Shaggy coats dripping, the bears dash and plunge about in the foaming water, grabbing and snapping after the pink-fleshed fish. The brown bears of Eurasia, rather mild-mannered and only a third the size of the big Alaskan breed, consume more plant matter than their relatives, and, in fact, some of the European strain are almost completely vegetarian.

Termites are a staple of the sloth bear (*Melursus ursinus*) of the Indian subcontinent and Sri Lanka, and to get at the insects this dim-sighted creature has evolved a snout that approximates a vacuum cleaner. The lips of the sloth bear are hairless and flexible and can be protruded like a tube a considerable distance from the mouth. The bear can also close its nostrils whenever it wishes. After digging open a termite mound, the bear literally huffs and puffs to uncover and ingest its prey. Puckering its lips into a tube, with its nostrils shut to keep out dust, it blows away the loose dirt to expose the termites, then sucks them in, a process facilitated by a gap in its teeth resulting from the absence of two upper incisors.

Two other tropical bears, the spectacled bear *(Tremarctos ornatus)* of South America and the little Malayan sun bear *(Helarctos malayanus)*, obtain much of their food from the trees. The spectacled bear, so called because of the light markings that ring its eyes, hauls its 300-pound body aloft to a true nest, but forages much on the ground for palm stalks, new leaves, and seeds. The sun bear—the only bear smaller than an average human being—lives in a tree nest and eats fruit and the soft young growth of coconut palms. The raccoons and their relatives are even more adept in the branches. Raccoons often nest in tree hollows and take refuge in the trees when pursued by dogs and hunters. Troops of coatis readily scramble from the ground into the boughs. The ringtail cats are able climbers, generally living and denning on rock cliff faces. Two other members of the family, the olingo *(Bassaricyon gabbii)* and the kinkajou *(Potos flavus)*, are the equal of monkeys in the trees. The two species, both residents of the American tropics, regularly associate with one another. They are night rovers, wide of eye, and quietly search the forest canopy for the fruit they relish above all else. Rather gregarious—although it is not so much sociability as the presence of juicy fruit that brings them together—the kinkajous and olingos are long-bodied animals, with long tails as well. The tail of the kinkajou, an animal that moves with deliberation through the treetops, is the ultimate adaptation to the arboreal world, for, like the tails of New World monkeys, it is prehensile, serving as anchor and fifth hand. Looking like a rust-colored raccoon, the lesser panda *(Ailurus fulgens)* of southwestern China and bordering lands further demonstrates the arboreal proclivities of the raccoon family. The little red panda sleeps in the trees by day, its brushy tail wrapped around its head like the tail of a sled dog in the snow, and although it generally forages on the ground, it uses the trees as a refuge and tree hollows as dens. Even the giant panda (*Ailuropoda melanoleuca*), as much a model for dolls and figurines as the "teddy bear" koala of Australia, will climb into the trees if pursued, although it can weigh upward of 300 pounds. Few mammals have caused so much difficulty for those people whose job it is to classify the members of the animal kingdom, assigning them to neat little groups. The giant panda is a source of puzzlement because it shares characteristics with more than one group. Taxonomists seem unable to agree whether it is a bear, a member of the raccoon family, or a bridge between the two groups. All they are sure of is that it is one of the three. The black-and-white panda has been a problem for the classifiers for only a century or so, because the world of Western science did not know of the creature until the late 1860s, when Jean Pierre Armand David, a Roman Catholic priest and naturalist, ventured into its rugged bamboo-covered territory in western China and Tibet and in all likelihood became the first European to see the creature. For the peoples of the West, David had found a new and curious animal. For the classifiers, he had created a problem that more than likely cannot be solved.

**59** *and* **60** *overleaf. The grizzly or brown bear* (Ursus arctos) *has been the center of many controversies ever since white man first intruded into its domain in the North American West. Most have been serious matters of survival for both bear and man. Not so the long-running battle over its name—or names. As one noted zoologist wrote, "Probably no other piece of research has brought dignified mammalogists nearer to name-calling and nose-punching than the question of correctly classifying the grizzly bear." The argument is between the "lumpers" and "splitters" in the taxonomic fraternity, which relies heavily on the shape of mammals' skulls and teeth in determining their classification. And the problem is the great variation in skulls and teeth among these big carnivores. Thus one scientist, a splitter in the extreme, decided there were eighty-four different species and sub-species of grizzly and brown bears in North America, and he claimed five distinct species could be found on one Alaskan island only a hundred miles long! Today, however, the lumpers rule. They tell us only a single species of brown bear is found across the entire Northern Hemisphere. Smallest of the local races is the 200-pound Syrian bear; largest of all is the Kodiak bear of coastal Alaska, a giant that stands nine feet tall on its hind legs and weighs 1600 pounds. All have that same ominous appearance—a hollowed-out face and a big hump between the shoulders. In North America, the term "grizzly" is given to the bears of the Rocky Mountain wilderness and inland Alaska, "brown bear" to those that haunt the Alaska coast, feeding on grass, berries, and other vegetable matter much of the year but growing fat in midsummer on the salmon that pack rivers and creeks on spawning runs from the sea.* (59 Stephen J. Krasemann/DRK Photo; 60 Fred Bruemmer)

**64** *overleaf. Stalking the pack ice and frigid waters around the North Pole in search of seals and walruses, the polar bear* (Ursus maritimus) *is one of the great nomads of the mammal kingdom. It spends most of its life at sea, often floating hundreds of miles from land on great ice floes. A powerful swimmer, the polar bear has front paws that are partially webbed, and the soles of its broad feet are furred for insula-tion against the cold and to provide traction. Polar bears come ashore only occasionally, varying their diet with tundra berries or hunting down a caribou or musk-ox. In winter, females make a snow den on land to give birth to their cubs, which number from one to four.* (Fred Baldwin/National Audubon Society Collection/Photo Researchers, Inc.)

**62.** *Although the giant panda* (Ailuropoda melanoleuca) *is a symbol of wildlife conservation around the world, its life in the mountain forests of China remains a mystery more than a century after its discovery. Scientists know that the giant panda eats copious amounts of bamboo shoots, a food with low nutritional value, and that its striking black-and-white coloration is an effective camouflage as the 300-pound animal sits on its haunches high in a tree. But what little else is known about panda behavior has been gained from studies of the very few animals in zoos.* (Jean-Paul Ferrero)

**63.** *A family of lesser pandas* (Ailurus fulgens), *long-tailed Asian members of the raccoon family. The lesser panda frequents the mountain forests and bamboo thickets on the south-facing slopes of the Himalayas, from Nepal to Burma and the Chinese provinces of Yunnan and Szechwan. It too feeds extensively on bamboo, grasping the shoots with prehensile thumbs and chewing the tough fiber with powerful jaws and large teeth. But unlike the giant panda, it is not strictly vegetarian, for it eats nestling birds, eggs, rodents, and insects captured on its nocturnal ventures.* (George Holton)

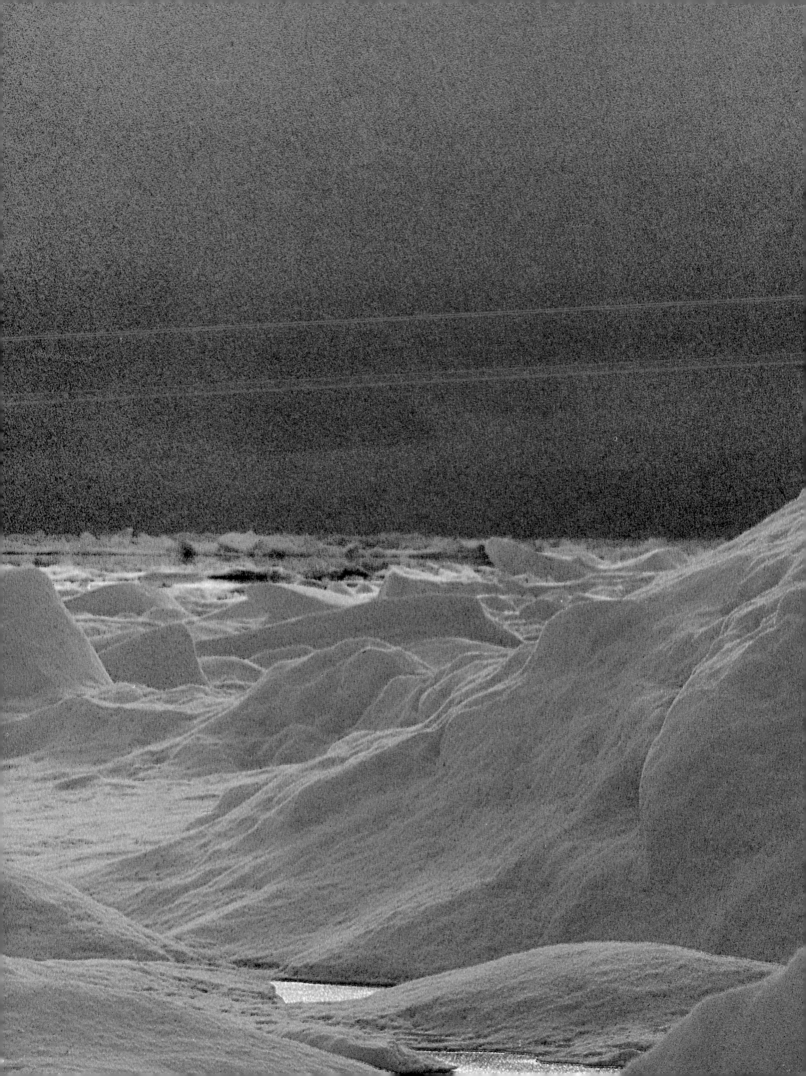

Watching a great whale rise from the depths of a calm sea is like witnessing the birth of an island. One moment the sea is smooth, stirred only by light swells that slide gently across its surface, or perhaps by the occasional splash of a seabird knifing into the water after a fish. Then the ocean parts. A dark and mountainous form, encrusted with a white mottling of barnacles, heaves above the surface. Water drains in torrents from the crest of its back and sluices into the foam boiling around it. Overhead, like clouds of steam above a volcano, hangs the condensation from the sea beast's exhalations, which fill the air with a mighty rushing sound. It is an experience to make one feel fragile and insignificant, and to prompt pondering about man's place on earth.

The great whales are the most spectacular of a group of mammals that have adapted to the world of water. This assemblage also includes the smaller whales, dolphins, and porpoises, the seals and their kin, and the dugongs and manatees. In a sense, they have come full circle, for they have returned to the environment from which their remote cold-blooded ancestors crept and, indeed, from which all life arose. Most of them are marine, but a few, such as the weak-eyed river dolphins (Platanistidae) of Asia and South America, and Siberia's Lake Baikal seal *(Pusa sibirica)*, spend their lives in fresh water. Although the mammals here belong to three unrelated orders, they share a parallel history. For reasons only to be surmised, the ancestors forsook the land and committed themselves to life in the water—probably because the pressures of competition or the

# Mammals in the Sea

need for a new source of food forced them to.
The whales, dolphins, and porpoises—together called cetaceans—made the transition in the Eocene Period, at the dawn of the Age of Mammals more than 45 million years ago. The dugongs and manatees, comprising the order of sirenians, accomplished it at about the same time. Not for another 20 million years, in the Miocene Period, did the seals and their relatives appear in the sea. They are sometimes grouped together in a single order, the pinnipeds—meaning "wing-footed"—but all of them may not have evolved from the same ancestors. The true seals, streamlined for swimming to the degree that they have lost external ears, possibly hark back to an otter-like ancestor. The fur seals, sea lions, and walruses, on the other hand, may descend from creatures close to bears.
The sirenians probably arose from the same rootstock as the elephants, but the origin of the whales and their cousins is elusive. Students of evolution have seen in the cetaceans signs pointing back both to carnivorous ancestors and herbivores. Some of the earliest whales had teeth similar to archaic meat eaters. Yet chemical analysis shows that modern cetaceans contain some proteins similar to those in sheep, cattle, and camels. No matter what ancestors produced the cetaceans and the other animals considered here, any resemblances they have to distant kin on land are only fleeting echoes of ancient relationships. The pinnipeds, for instance, may be offshoots of the carnivores, but living in the water has sufficiently reshaped the seals and the rest of their flippered band to confer upon them a distinct

identity. The ways in which such creatures have adapted to life beyond the world's shorelines merit profound consideration, if not awe, because they all have managed to cope with an environment almost as hostile to a mammal as the cold blackness of space.

As a matter of course, these animals go for long periods without breathing the air upon which they, like all other mammals, depend. The sirenians sometimes stay below for a quarter of an hour as they pull eelgrass, water hyacinths, and other aquatic plants into their small mouths with the aid of a fleshy and flexible upper lip. The sea otter *(Enhydra lutris)* scours the bottom down to one hundred feet, probing with stubby forepaws for the shellfish and sea urchins it relishes. A month-old harbor seal *(Phoca vitulina)* can dive for up to four minutes on a single breath. A yearling of the same species can hold its breath for twenty minutes. The southern elephant seal *(Mirounga leonina)*, a giant twenty feet long weighing up to 8000 pounds, need not come up for a half hour after it dives. The Weddell seal *(Leptonychotes weddelli)*, a 900-pound beast of the south polar regions, spends more than half the year in the sea under several feet of ice, and sometimes must hold its breath for an hour as it travels miles between breathing holes. This seal customarily cruises at depths approaching 1000 feet, but it may dive to twice that depth. The legendary sperm whale *(Physeter catodon)* routinely searches the dim reaches 1500 feet down for squid and not rarely descends to almost 3000 feet. Several years ago, one of these behemoths was found entangled in a transoceanic cable at 3200 feet. When necessary, as in a titanic battle with a huge squid, a sperm whale can remain under for an hour and a half. Whales may stay down longer and range even deeper than we suspect, for although they have been pursued over the surface by humans for centuries, we really know very little about how they behave beneath the waves.

To remain under very long without breathing, a sea mammal must use oxygen with exceptional economy, and in fact this ability is one of the traits unifying the orders which have left the land behind. The sirenians and whales promote oxygen conservation with their relatively low metabolism. In terms of calories per kilogram of body weight, the basic metabolic rate of a whale is one-fifteenth that of a human, and the blood of a typical whale holds sufficient oxygen to keep its bodily processes going for more than an hour. Moreover, the deep-living sea mammals have a generous supply of blood for their size. A seal, for example, has one and a half times as much as a land mammal of equal bulk. Sea mammals also have an abundance of myoglobin, the oxygen-carrying protein that serves the same function in the muscles as hemoglobin in the blood. It all means that their bodies store vast amounts of oxygen.

Even more telling is the astonishing efficiency with which sea mammals operate during a dive. They reduce, even shut off, all bodily activities not essential beneath the surface of the water. By selected constriction of the blood vessels, the flow to the kidneys and digestive system, for example, is slowed drastically, while blood continues to rush unimpeded to the brain, spinal cord, and heart muscles. Thus the oxygen in the blood is reserved for the organs which must function during the dive. At the same time, the heartbeat decreases; in the bottle-nose dolphin *(Tursiops truncatus)*, for instance, it is reduced to as much as half the normal rate. When the gray seal *(Halichoerus grypus)* dives, its heart beats 10 times a minute, as compared with 100 to 150 times a minute at the surface. Beyond this, the sea mammals seem rather insensitive to the buildup of carbon dioxide, which in land mammals quickly triggers impulses in the respiratory center of the brain that result in the act of taking breath.

The ability to clamp the nostrils tightly shut underwater, closing off the respiratory system, is an enormous advantage for a mammal in the water. For this purpose, the nostrils of pinnipeds are narrow slits. Those of the sirenians and cetaceans are round orifices ringed by a muscular rim. During the course of evolution, some major rearranging was also accomplished in the nasal tract of the cetaceans. The nostrils have been moved from the snout to the apex of the head, forming a single blowhole in the toothed whales, paired in the baleen whales. As a result, a whale can breathe with only the tip of its head above the surface. Underwater, a whale opens its mouth without danger of drowning, because the nasal and throat passages are separated, so that the lungs open to the outside only through the blowhole. Many other changes, some quite obvious, have occurred in those mammals that truly have made the water their home. Most recognizable is that they have taken on the so-called fusiform body shape typical of fish, at its sleekest, perhaps, in creatures such as the killer whale (*Orcinus orca*). Even such bulky and ponderous animals as the walrus (*Odobenus rosmarus*) and dugong (*Dugong dugon*) streamline into a torpedo shape as they move through the water. The blubber that insulates them smooths out, reshaping their lumpy outlines into symmetrical contours. The density of water has had other influences on the sea mammals. The support provided by water has allowed some of them to reach enormous size. Only the aquatic environment could produce an animal with a body more than 100 feet long, weighing 170 tons. That creature is the blue whale (*Balaenoptera musculus*), the largest animal that has ever lived. Ironically, the blue whale may vanish because of its size, which, marked this mighty sea mammal as a prime target of whalers—men as rapacious as any of the beasts under the sea.

71. *Using its powerful forelegs for propulsion, a Galápagos fur seal* (Arctocephalus australis galapagoensis) *plunges into a grotto on James Bay, on San Salvador Island. The fur seals that bred in immense numbers on islands around the Southern Hemisphere were nearly annihilated in the nineteenth century, slaughtered for their treasured pelts. In the first two years after their discovery, for example, 600,000 sealskins went to market from the South Shetland Islands. In 1821, a single ship arriving in London from Antarctic sealing grounds carried 400,000 pelts. What saved most of the several species of southern fur seals was economics: two few remained to make further harvests profitable. In the case of the Galápagos fur seal, the fact that a few individuals retreated into lava caves in daytime prevented its extinction.* (Soames Summerhays/National Audubon Society Collection/Photo Researchers, Inc.)

72 *overleaf. This bull Steller's sea lion* (Eumetopias jubata), *surrounded by his harem, is ten feet long and weighs 2000 pounds. Grown fat on a diet of fish, this inhabitant of Pacific beaches from the Aleutian Islands of Alaska to Japan and California is the largest of several species of sea lions. It is named for Georg Wilhelm Steller, the German who was the first naturalist to reach Alaska in the eighteenth century.* (Edward R. Degginger)

74 *second overleaf. At sunset on Hood Island, a Galápagos sea lion bull and cow* (Zalophus californianus wollebaeki) *luxuriate in the falling spray from a blowhole. Like fur seals, sea lions belong to the family of eared seals. They can stand on four "legs" and almost gallop on land.* (Ron Church/TOM STACK & ASSOCIATES)

**76** *top left. Sea lions soak up the equatorial sun burning down on the Galápagos lava. Unlike fur seals, sea lions were not hunted primarily for their pelts, since their coat has no underfur. Instead, they were slaughtered for food and rendered for oil and their skins were processed into low-grade leather.* (George Holton)

**76** *bottom left. The aptly named leopard seal (Hydrurga leptonyx) patrols Antarctic ice floes, waiting for Adélie penguins to enter the water. Its prey is quickly dispatched, shaken out of its skin, and swallowed whole. So fierce that they are avoided even by packs of killer whales, leopard seals are longer than all other seals except the elephant seal.* (William Curtsinger/National Audubon Society Collection/Photo Researchers, Inc.)

**76** *top right. Harp seals (Phoca groenlandicus) are true seals that move on land only with considerable difficulty. Their annual oceanic migrations cover 6000 miles and scientists calculate that a harp seal must consume a ton and a half of fish and crustaceans to fuel its journey. Harp seals bear their young on pack ice off the coasts of Labrador, Newfoundland, and Greenland, and the slaughter of newborn pups for their pure-white coats is a continuing source of international controversy.* (Fred Bruemmer)

**6** *bottom right. Soon after the birth of her single pup, which weighs less than five pounds, a sea lion cow will mate again. The pups, which bleat like lambs, spend their first three months nursing and frolicking in tidal pools. The mortality rate is high: pups often fall into the sea, are unable to scramble back onto the rocks, and drown; others are crushed by bulls fighting over a harem of ten to twenty cows.* (ANIMALS ANIMALS/© Michael and Barbara Reed)

**77.** *Skilled swimmers, sea lions can dive to depths of more than 300 feet and remain submerged for fifteen minutes. But deadly enemies are waiting offshore: sharks and killer whales.* (Carl Roessler/ Sea Library)

**78** *overleaf. Young bull elephant seals* (Mirounga leonina) *gather in a knotlike formation on a beach in the South Shetland Islands, between Cape Horn and Antarctica. Easier to kill than a whale, these blubbery monsters—a mature bull may carry four tons of weight on its fifteen-foot hulk—once were butchered by the tens of thousands and boiled down for their oil.* (George Holton)

**80.** *With surprising agility, a bull elephant seal has dragged itself to the luxury of its mud wallow on Campbell Island, south of New Zealand. On the breeding grounds, old bulls have a busy time keeping possession of the much smaller and faster cows in the harem, for the opportunistic younger bulls in the vicinity are always awaiting a chance to mate with unguarded cows.* (George Holton)

**81.** *The northern elephant seal* (Mirounga angustirostris) *of California waters nearly passed into extinction in the 1890s. By the time it was given complete protection from hunting, fewer than 100 animals survived. Today there are 15,000 on the Channel Islands off Los Angeles. The northern species has a longer "trunk" than its Antarctic cousin— that snout that dangles limp most of the year but is inflated during the excitement of the mating season.*

*Elephant seals haul out on land twice a year—once to breed, and again a few weeks later to molt. While ashore they fast, living off their great fat reserves built up by feasting on cuttlefish and squid caught in the ocean depths.* (Bob Evans/ Sea Library)

**83.** *Their skin baked red by the Arctic sun, walruses sprawl across a rocky island in the Bering Strait separating Alaska from Siberia. The hide of a walrus may be an inch thick, and is so tough it was used in the construction of the Cologne cathedral in Germany in the thirteenth century.* (Fred Bruemmer)

**82.** *The ivory tusks of a walrus* (Odobenus rosmarus) *grow throughout the animal's life, and those of a mature male can reach a length of forty inches and weigh twelve pounds. The walrus uses its tusks to haul its two-ton hulk out of the sea and as a weapon—and possibly to dig out mollusks from the floor of the ocean.* (George Holton)

**84** *overleaf. Two walrus calves nuzzle each other, showing the stiff bristles that, when they begin to fend for themselves after nursing for two years, will be an important tool in feeding. A walrus has a mustache of some four hundred sensitive bristles that are used not only to rake up food on the muddy bottom but also to hold a mollusk shell while the animal is sucked out. A young calf will cling to the back of its mother with its front flippers as she dives after food, and in this position it may be vulnerable to an attack by killer whales. But walruses have few enemies other than man; polar bears sometimes kill calves on land or ice, but are no match for protective mothers in water.* (Jean-Phillipe Varin/Jacana)

**88** *overleaf.* A common dolphin (Delphinus delphis) *races alongside a yacht in the Galápagos Islands. Eight feet long, capable of attaining a speed of 30 miles an hour, this is truly the common dolphin of temperate seas around the world; herds of* Delphinus *numbering in the thousands can literally churn the ocean to froth as they pursue squid, baitfish, and flying fish.* (Nicholas DeVore III/Bruce Coleman, Inc.)

**86.** *A 1500-pound northern manatee* (Trichechus manatus) *can remain submerged for sixteen minutes as it feasts on aquatic vegetation. It pushes plants toward its mouth with its flippers, picks them up with a split lip that is used like a forceps, and works the food into its mouth with the stiff bristles on its muzzle. In cold weather, Florida manatees congregate around warmer springs in rivers and even city water outlets in Miami.* (Ron Church/TOM STACK & ASSOCIATES)

**87.** *Floating on its back in California's Monterey Bay, a sea otter* (Enhydra lutris) *is impervious to the sharp spines of the sea urchin on which it is feeding. Sea otters are a rarity among mammals: they use tools! To smash open the hard shells of mollusks, the otter lays a stone on its chest and uses it like an anvil. The stone is then carried under the otter's arm as it dives as deep as 130 feet in search of another clam, snail, or urchin.* (Jeffrey Foott/Bruce Coleman, Inc.)

**92** *overleaf. In a burst of spray, a right whale* (Balaena glacialis) *explodes from a bay off Punta Váldez on the coast of Argentina, hurling itself into the air with such momentum that it somersaults. A whale will breach repeatedly, a score or more times, always landing on its back or side with a thunderous whack. Just why whales breach is not understood; it may be done to dislodge parasites—or just for sport.* (Jen and Des Bartlett/Bruce Coleman, Inc.)

**90.** *In the clear waters off the Hawaiian island of Maui, a calf humpback whale* (Megaptera novae-angliae) *stays close by the side of its mother. Some two hundred of these rare whales, famous for their "singing," use the warm near-shore waters of Hawaii as a mating ground and as a nursery, remaining there from February to June, when they depart for nutrient-rich feeding grounds in cold northern seas.* (James Hudnall)

**91.** *Each wartlike knob on the head of this humpback calf contains a single sensitive vibrissa that is similar to a cat's whisker. The baby whale, sixteen feet long at birth, is not yet parasitized by the barnacles that bedeck adult humpbacks —as much as a half ton of them affixed to a single whale.* (James Hudnall)

# Notes on Photographers

**Durward L. Allen** (31), veteran wildlife photographer, is a Professor of Wildlife Ecology at Purdue University.

**Fred Baldwin** (64) lives in Georgia and specializes in photographing the southeastern United States and the Arctic.

**Jen and Des Bartlett** (92) are Australians known for their wildlife films (including the notable *Flight of the Snow Goose*) and for stills made on every continent.

**Wolfgang Bayer** (48) is a wildlife film producer who has made television films for the National Geographic Society, Walt Disney Productions, and *Wild World of Animals*.

**Rajesh Bedi** (40) is a New Delhi photographer whose photographs of Indian wildlife have appeared in international publications.

**Stanley Breeden** (25, 39) has photographed wildlife throughout the world. His pictures have been published in numerous international publications.

**Fred Bruemmer** (60, 76, 83) was a newspaper photographer and reporter in Canada before becoming a freelancer specializing in the Arctic. He has written 300 articles and five books, including *The Arctic*.

**Fred and Dora Burris** (14) are writer-photographers whose work has appeared in many national magazines, including *Audubon*.

**Ron Church** (74, 86) was cinematographer for the original Jacques Cousteau television series. He was also pilot of the Westinghouse Deepstar three-man research submarine.

**Jack Couffer** (18) is a cinematographer whose credits include Walt Disney's True Life Series and *Jonathan Livingston Seagull*, for which he was nominated for an Academy Award.

**Bill Curtsinger** (76) is a contract photographer for the National Geographic Society, specializing in marine mammal photography.

**Edward R. Degginger** (43, 72) is both a professional chemist and a photographer of wildlife. Over 3600 of his pictures have appeared in books, magazines and encyclopedias.

**Nicholas DeVore III** (88) freelances for the National Geographic Society. Born in Paris, he now lives near Aspen, Colorado.

**John Ebeling** (17, 30) is a Minnesota-based nature photographer who is much concerned with protecting porcupines. His pictures have been published in *National Wildlife*.

**Bob Evans** (81) is a nature and underwater photographer living in Santa Barbara, California. He heads his own production company, La Mer Bleu.

**Jean-Paul Ferrero** (62) is a French wildlife photographer whose work has been published in numerous European books and periodicals.

**Kenneth Fink** (13) became interested in photographing mammals while working for the U.S. National Park Service. He teaches public school in San Diego, California.

**Jeffrey Foott** (87) is a biologist studying marine mammal behavior. His pictures of wildlife have appeared in *Audubon*, *National Geographic*, and in Chanticleer Press books.

**George Holton** (1, 63, 76, 78, 80, 82) was a New York based photographer whose work appeared in publications of the Audubon Society, the National Geographic Society and Time-Life Books. His travels took him to nearly every part of the world.

**Maurice Hornocker** (43) began photographing animals while he was a student at the University of Montana. His photographs have appeared in several national publications.